Succes...

Great Litt...
Successful Selling

By
Brian Tracy

AMRIT BOOK CO. ☎ 3317331
.Books on India. History, Politics, Philosophy,
Religion, Computer - Management,
All   Cometitive   Examinations.
21-N, Conn. Circus New Delhi-1

JAICO PUBLISHING HOUSE
Mumbai • Delhi • Bangalore
Kolkata • Hyderabad • Chennai

© 1997 by Career Press

No part of this book may be reproduced or utilized in any form or by any means, electronic or mechanical including photocopying, recording or by any information storage and retrieval system, without permission in writing from the publishers.

Published in arrangement with:
Career Press, Inc., 3 Tice Road, P.O. Box 687,
Franklin Lakes, NJ 07417.

GREAT LITTLE BOOK ON SUCCESSFUL SELLING
ISBN 81-7224-710-9

First Jaico Impression : 1999
Second Jaico Impression : 2000
Third Jaico Impression : 2002

Published by:
Jaico Publishing House
121, Mahatma Gandhi Road
Mumbai - 400 023.

Printed by:
Paras Printing Press
123, Adhyaru Ind. Estate, Sun Mill Compound,
Lower Parel, Mumbai - 400 013.

Pattern yourself after the very best people in your field. Do what they do.

Keep yourself positive, cheerful and goal-oriented. Sales success is 80 percent attitude and only 20 percent aptitude.

Combine the dual qualities of empathy and ambition in every sales relationship.

If it's worth doing, it's worth doing poorly at first. Don't be afraid to try.

Develop the "winning edge" in sales. Small differences in ability can translate into enormous differences in results.

Guard your thoughts carefully. The quality of your thinking determines the quality of your life.

Think continually of yourself as if you were one of the top money earners in your field. How would you think, talk, and behave if you were already there?

Keep your mind positive at all times. Interpret things to yourself in a positive way.

In every sales situation, act boldly and unseen forces will come to your aid.

Think of the amount of money you want to earn this year and then imagine that you are already at that level.

Continually push yourself out of your comfort zone. Push yourself to stretch as you try new things each day.

Think before you act and then act decisively. Fortune favors the brave.

Develop a clear blueprint for sales success, covering every aspect of your activities.

Refuse to let the fear of rejection hold you back. Remember, rejection is never personal.

Get around the winners in selling. Associate with the very best people in your industry and avoid the others.

Make a habit of dominating the listening and let the customer dominate the talking.

Accept complete responsibility for everything you are and everything you ever will be. Because you are responsible.

Position yourself as a consultant rather than a salesperson, first in your own mind and then in the mind of your customer.

Approach each customer with the idea of helping him or her solve a problem or achieve a goal, not of selling a product or service.

Resolve to be among the top 20 percent of salespeople who make 80 percent of the sales.

Familiarize yourself with every detail of what you sell and what your competitors sell as well.

Be positive, pleasant, patient and easygoing—
no matter how busy you really are.

Whatever got you to where you are today is
not enough to keep you there.

Learn to use the telephone professionally and
skillfully as an essential business tool.

Think of yourself as a resource to yourself and to your clients, an advisor, counselor, mentor and friend.

Plan your work and work your plan. Decide in advance exactly how you are going to get from where you are to where you want to go.

Become a strategic thinker. Set goals for what you want and create organized plans of action to achieve them.

Be intensely result-oriented in everything you do. This is a key characteristic of high performers.

Be sensitive to the best interests of your customers, but never forget that you are there to sell, not socialize.

Practice the Golden Rule in selling: "Sell unto others as you would have them sell unto you."

Use testimonial letters from satisfied customers at every opportunity.

Practice the Law of Indirect Effort in selling; concentrate on the relationship and the sale will usually take care of itself.

Refuse to make excuses or blame others for anything in your life or work. This is the mark of the superior person.

A person will not buy from you until he is convinced that you are a friend and are acting in his best interest. You must make this clear.

Never criticize, condemn or complain in a conversation with a customer or prospect.

Build the self-esteem of your customer by listening attentively and showing respect for his thoughts and opinions.

Play your own game; plan your selling process and then follow your plan.

Guard your integrity as a sacred thing; nothing is as important as the integrity of your own mind.

Measure the value of everything you do against the sales results that are expected of you.

Dedicate yourself to building and maintaining high-quality selling relationships with every prospect and customer.

Give your own personal guarantees of satisfaction in addition to those of your company.

Satisfy the deep subconscious needs of your customers—to feel important, to feel valued, respected and worthwhile.

Develop an "attitude of gratitude." Say thank you to everyone you meet for everything they do for you.

Show that your product or service provides the exact benefit that your customer is seeking and is ideally priced for what it does.

Talk optimistically about the future of your business or your industry. Keep your doubts and concerns to yourself.

Your life can only get better when you do. Do something every day to improve in your key skill areas.

Never assume you understand the customer's concerns. Question for clarification. Ask, "How do you mean, exactly?" and wait for the answer.

Be upbeat, optimistic and encouraging in all your interactions with others. Remember, everyone you meet is carrying a heavy load.

You create a customer by convincing him overwhelmingly that you are the lowest-risk, highest-value, easiest person and company to do business with.

Identify the "fatal flaw" in your sales performance; what is holding you back?

Aspire greatly; anything less than a commitment to excellence becomes an acceptance of mediocrity.

Be open to constructive criticism from others; it's the only way you can learn and grow.

You determine your future by the thoughts and pictures you hold in your mind today.

Don't be afraid to try new ideas in selling. Try something new several times before you pass judgment on it.

You keep customers by delivering on your promises, fulfilling your commitments and continually investing in the quality of your relationships.

Learn to concentrate single-mindedly on the most important thing that you can be doing at any one time.

Move out of your comfort zone. You can only grow if you are willing to feel awkward and uncomfortable when you try something new.

Allocate your time carefully. Spend it with people who can buy from you within a reasonable period of time.

Measure your performance in a critical area against someone who is doing very well in that area. Use that performance as your standard.

Clarify the most pressing single problem that your product or service can solve.

Preparation is the mark of the professional. Take the time to go over every detail in advance of meeting the customer.

Identify the primary objections to your product offering and then develop bulletproof answers to those objections.

Develop the healthy personality and resilient attitude that is vital to sales success. You can if you think you can.

"Intensity of Purpose" is the distinguishing characteristic of all outstanding men and women. It requires clear goals, burning desire and relentless persistence.

Dream big! There are no limits to how good you can become or how high you can rise except the limits you put on yourself.

Discipline yourself to plan and organize every hour of every day before you begin.

Get serious about your career; decide today to be a big success in everything you do.

Imagine that your limitations exist only in your mind, and think about what you would do if they did not exist at all.

You become what you think about most of the time. Keep your mind on what you want instead of what you don't want.

Be absolutely clear about what you want, why you want it, when you want it and what you are willing to do to get it.

Discipline yourself to spend more time with those people who represent the highest potential payoff.

Set excellent performance as your standard and strive to achieve it each day.

You have the same mental potential as anyone else; it is only what you choose to do with it that determines the course of your life.

You always tend to reap what you sow. You are reaping today exactly what you have sown in the past. How do you like it?

Decide exactly what you want in life and then do the same things that others have done to achieve the same results.

Take the long view. Don't let short-term setbacks disturb you.

Everything you have in your life today you have attracted to yourself because of the person you are.

Decide upon your values as a sales professional and refuse to compromise them for anyone, or for any reason.

Talk to yourself positively all the time; say, "I feel happy! I feel healthy! I feel terrific!"

Superior salespeople don't really compete with others, they compete with their own past performances.

Whatever you dwell upon expands and grows in your life. What do you think about most of the time and where is this taking you?

There are a thousand excuses for every failure, but never a good reason. What are your favorite excuses for holding yourself back?

Concentrate single-mindedly on the things you want and the person you want to be. Block all other thoughts out of your mind.

Practice mental rehearsal prior to every sales call. Visualize prior success and imagine that you are about to enjoy it again.

Be thankful for all your blessings. An appreciative person makes a pleasant and optimistic person.

Dream big dreams. Make out a list of everything that you could ever want, exactly as if you had no limitations.

Ask your way to success; the future belongs to the "askers."

Analyze your current situation. What do you have to do today to get to where you want to be in the future?

Write out a mission statement for yourself as a sales professional. Make it a present tense description of your ideal life sometime in the future.

Demonstrate to your customer the difference between price and cost. The price is what it takes to purchase the item. The cost is the amount the customer eventually pays. They are not the same.

Become comfortable with silence. Don't talk while your customer is thinking about your offer.

Practice "back-from-the-future" thinking. Imagine that five years have passed and you have achieved all your goals. Describe your life at that time.

Practice the "reality principle"; deal with the world as it is, not as you wish it would be.

Deploy yourself carefully
to maximum advantage;
always invest your
energies where you can
get the highest return.

The amount you are worth today, divided by the amount of years you have been working, tells you how much you have traded your years for so far.

Describe your product in terms of what it "does," not in terms of what it "is."

You will always be compensated in direct proportion to the value of your contribution. If you want to get more out, you must put more in.

Design your ideal home in every respect; determine how much it will cost and how long it will take you to acquire it.

Tune in to your customer's favorite radio station, WIIFM: "What's in it for me?"

Analyze the trends in your industry and your career. Where are you likely to be in three to five years?

Make a list of all the reasons you want to be a major success in your field; reasons are the fuel in the furnace of achievement.

Apply "zero-based thinking" to every part of your life; what would you not get into today if you had it to do over?

Listen to stress and use it as a friend to tell you what parts of your life are out of alignment with your true nature.

Dress conservatively for maximum credibility in any business situation.

Imagine that you have no limitations on what you can be, have or do. If you were completely free to choose, what changes would you make in your life?

Deal honestly and objectively with yourself; intellectual honesty and personal courage are the hallmarks of great character.

Expand your vocabulary; learn and use new and better words every day.

Identify your weakest skill area, and make a plan to become very good in that one skill that is holding you back.

Get the feeling; imagine that you have already succeeded before you go in.

Invite feedback from others on your performance; you can only get better when people will evaluate you honestly and tell you what they see.

Stand in front of a full-length mirror every morning and ask yourself if you see a top professional looking back at you.

Know your product cold; learn it inside out. Product knowledge builds self-confidence and personal power.

Develop your assets. Your most valuable asset is your reputation, how you are known to your customers.

Face the facts; ask your last 10 noncustomers why they didn't buy from you.

Develop a meaningful competitive advantage as a salesperson; what do you have the potential to do better than anyone else?

Develop trust with your customers by asking good questions and listening attentively to the answers.

Commit yourself to becoming one of the outstanding sales professionals of your generation.

Win in competitive markets by continually analyzing your competition, and by positioning your product as the superior choice.

Help your customer to identify his or her real needs before you ever mention your product or service.

Never assume you understand what your customer has just said; paraphrase and feed it back to him in your own words.

Never come across as impatient; always be relaxed, cheerful and positive—even if you're all wound up inside.

Do your own market research; ask your last 10 customers exactly why they bought from you.

View your prospect as if you were a doctor and he was a patient; do a thorough examination and diagnosis before you recommend a prescription.

Approach selling as a profession, like law or medicine. See yourself at the same level as the best people in your community.

Offer your customers a long-term relationship, then do everything possible to build and maintain it.

Present your product or service as an improvement on what the customer is already doing. Remember that people are fearful of change.

Don't be afraid to ask, "Why don't you give it a try?"

Develop wisdom in sales by reflecting on your experience and learning everything you can from every call.

Be an agreeable person; never argue with a customer, even if he or she appears to be dead wrong.

Remember, rule number one in selling is, "The customer is always right." Rule number two is, "When in doubt, refer back to rule number one."

Arrive punctually for every appointment; if you are not early, you're late. Always give yourself a cushion of 10 minutes.

Express your admiration for the traits, possessions or accomplishments of your customer. Little things mean a lot.

Introduce the continuous improvement process into every aspect of your sales work; resolve to become better, in some way, every day.

Always give people the choice of "A" or "B" rather than "Yes" or "No."

Keep your sales pipeline full by prospecting continually. Always have more people to see than you have time to see them.

Always be willing to go the extra mile, to do more than is expected of you. There are never any traffic jams on the extra mile.

Focus your sales conversation on the benefits that the customer will enjoy when he or she owns and uses your product or service.

Ask someone to accompany you on your sales calls, sit there quietly, and then tell you afterwards what they saw. Ask for feedback; you can only improve with the frank and honest evaluations of others.

Look upon your sales territory as a farmer looks upon a rich piece of land; like an area to be harvested, year after year.

Unlock your inborn creativity; always be looking for better, faster, easier ways to sell more of your product or service.

Prepare your questions thoroughly in advance; they are the keys to sales success.

Avoid negative people at all costs; they tire you out and wear you down.

Dedicate yourself to serving your customers and your sales will take care of themselves.

Determine the real reasons that people buy your product or service and organize your entire sales presentation around them.

Recognize the words, "I'm not interested," for what they are. The customer is saying that his or her interest has not yet been aroused sufficiently. That's all.

Listen for emotion-charged words that the customer uses; repeat them back later to show you were really listening.

Ask questions and listen until you discover the "hot button" of your customer; then structure your presentation around your client's concern.

Demonstrate that your product or service is the ideal solution to your client's problem. The sale follows from that.

Make a list of all the reasons why anyone would buy your product or service. Organize them by priority and memorize them.

Go to bed early each night; selling is hard work.

Don't use words like, "Quality," "Service," "Value," or "Price" as reasons to buy unless your competitors do not offer them at all. Otherwise, you'll just sound foolish.

Identify the attributes of an excellent prospect and then seek out more of them.

Help your customer recognize that he has an immediate need for what you are selling. This comes first.

Differentiate your product or service from your competitors' by emphasizing your "unique selling proposition." Bring the entire decision to hang on this key benefit.

Appeal to the most pressing need of your customer as it relates to your product in every selling situation.

Don't ever settle for less than your best; your potential is unlimited.

Give customers honest information about how your product or service can help them to improve their businesses or lives.

Determine the key result areas of your prospect; how can you help him or her to perform better in one of these areas?

Think about your easiest sales; why did they take place, and how could you create more of them?

Commit to being among the top 10 percent of people in your profession. Anything less is not worthy of you.

Dress the way your prospect's advisors dress; if you want people to accept your recommendations, you must look believable.

Pay twice as much for your clothes, and buy half as many. Expensive clothes are cheaper because you wear them more often.

Never wear or carry anything that looks cheap when you go to see a customer. It undermines your credibility.

Become an unshakable optimist; talk about and think about only the things you want.

Exercise regularly; the fitter you are, the more effective you will be.

Manage and influence the customer's perceptions of you by managing and influencing what you allow him or her to see and hear.

Start by sitting up straight, be alert and lean forward when you are talking to a customer. This makes you look professional.

Adopt the same body posture and positioning as your customer. This causes him to relax and be comfortable with you.

Think before you speak, and then speak clearly and distinctly. Face the customer directly, lean forward, smile and relax.

Be courteous and polite with everyone you meet when you are selling; you can never tell who has the real power.

Shake hands firmly; look him or her in the eye and say, "How do you do?"

Go slow at the beginning; seek first to understand, and then to be understood.

Become excellent at prospecting to overcome your fear of it. Inability to prospect is a major reason for sales failure.

List three reasons why a prospect should buy from you personally rather than from someone else.

Complete the sentence: "I could sell all I wanted if only my prospects didn't say..."

Listen to audiocassettes in your car; turn your car into a mobile "learning machine."

Become great in selling by spending more time with better prospects; how could you do this?

Join the business organizations and associations that are important to your industry. This can really pay off.

Recognize that value has a different meaning to different types of decision-makers.

Refuse to make excuses for failure; instead, look for the valuable lessons you can learn each time.

Read one hour per day to become better in selling; study the best that's ever been written.

Get around positive people; associate with the most successful salespeople in your field.

Develop a workaholic mentality; don't socialize or waste time.

Throw yourself wholeheartedly into your work; the more you enjoy it, the better you get.

Become excellent at telephone prospecting; learn to play the telephone like a musical instrument.

Be teachable; always assume that there is vital information you still need to learn.

Practice "creative procrastination." Put off calling on low-value, low-probability prospects and customers.

Use your time wisely; focus your energies where you can achieve major results.

Analyze your competition thoroughly; be clear about where you are strong and they are weak.

Identify the primary reasons that people do not buy from you; how could you remove these obstacles?

Identify your "limiting step" to sales success; what's holding you back?

Treat objections as requests for further information.

Compliment every objection by saying, "That's a good question."

Use the telephone like a business tool; get on and off fast.

Hear your customer out completely, no matter how many times you've heard the same things before.

Attend every sales seminar available; the highest paid are the best educated in their field.

Launch your new sales career by making 100 sales calls as fast as you can. Don't worry about selling anything.

Be truthful with your customers; tell them who you are and who you represent up-front.

Visualize yourself performing at your best in every sales situation.

Inhale and exhale deeply several times before every sales presentation to relax yourself.

Wait quietly for answers to your questions; be comfortable with silence.

Sell strategically; follow a logical process from beginning to end.

Develop a sense of urgency; move fast on opportunities or problems.

Be intensely action-oriented; the faster you move, the more energy you have and the better you get.

Concentrate single-mindedly on one thing, the most valuable thing, and stay with it until it's complete.

Develop your willpower so that you can make yourself do what you should do, when you should do it, whether you feel like it or not.

Never consider the possibility of failure; as long as you persist, you will be successful.

Recognize and take advantage of the cycles and trends in your industry.

Plan every day in advance, preferably the night before. Plan every week in advance, as well.

Get moving; the more ground you cover, the more people you see, the more successful you will be.

Dedicate yourself to continuous personal and professional improvement. It's the key to your future.

Take time out every day for the important people in your life.

Think about how you can differentiate your product from every other similar product in the marketplace.

Simplify your presentation so that it is clear what the customer gets.

Show the customer how she gets more in use value than she pays in dollar value. This is the key to the sale.

Take excellent care of your physical health; energy and dynamism are what sells.

See yourself as a role model for others, the picture of the perfect salesperson.

Build a bridge; establish a common bond with your customer before you begin selling.

Rehearse your sales presentation over and over again in your own mind before you get face to face.

Practice and memorize key questions that you can use to control the sales conversation.

Upgrade your knowledge continually; buyers are more sophisticated today than ever before.

Be prepared to deal with price as a major factor in every sale.

Structure your presentation so that you appeal to the different interests of the different decision-makers involved.

Use understatement rather than exaggeration in describing your products; it's more believable.

Only discuss or describe your product or service on the phone if your customer can buy over the phone.

Believe in yourself and your ultimate ability to succeed.

Get your prospect involved in the presentation;
give her things to hold or to look at.

Arouse the desire to own your product or
service by emphasizing the benefits of it to
your customer.

Be flexible in dealing with different customers
with different personalities.

Adjust the rhythm and tempo of your presentation to stay in step with your customer.

Find out who the final decision-maker is and structure your offering so that it is appealing to that individual.

Look for a coach in every sale, someone who wants you to be successful in the account.

Put price in its place; ask if you can come back to it later.

Be a problem detective; look for customer problems that your product or service can solve.

Quantify the net dollar benefit to your customer of using your product or service.

Learn how to be an excellent prospector in any market, under any conditions.

Seek out successful companies or individuals who can be even better off with your product or service.

Ask questions continually to build rapport, increase trust and gain vital information.

Segment your customers and focus on those who can benefit the most, immediately, from what you are selling.

Identify and emphasize the nonprice factors of your product or service that will determine the sale.

Demonstrate that your product is the best choice for your customer, not the lowest price.

Analyze your customer's situation clearly before you suggest your product or service.

Position yourself as a profit improvement specialist when selling to businesses.

Be willing to invest your time and energy to win a large customer or large sale. Nothing ventured, nothing gained.

Treat everyone you meet like a million dollar customer; you never can tell.

Look for the gap between where your customer is today and where he could be with your products.

Make intangible benefits tangible by showing the financial impact your product or service can have.

Determine how much you want to earn per hour and never do anything that pays less than your desired hourly rate.

End every sales conversation with an advance to the next stage of the sale.

Use a consultative selling approach. Ask more questions when you sell a high-tech product to a low-tech customer.

Plan carefully; the more detailed your plans, the more likely your success.

Take the time to think carefully before replying to your customer's comments.

Leave nothing to chance in the sales process. The devil is in the details. Everything counts.

First impressions are lasting; give special thought to your dress, your grooming and your accessories.

Take charge of your career; the best way to predict your sales future is to create it.

Concentrate on the activities of prospecting, presenting and following-up; the sales will take care of themselves.

Prepare thoroughly; have everything you need to sell before you go out on a call.

Make out a dream list of everything you could want to be, have or do if you had no limitations.

Use your time well; make every minute count.

List 20 things you are going to do in the next 30 days to fast-start your sales career. Then take action on at least one of them.

Think positively; you always perform on the outside based on how you think on the inside.

Develop and maintain momentum by working continuously toward your sales goals every day.

Create images of success and affluence and visualize them repeatedly.

Control your suggestive environment; only allow positive messages to reach your subconscious mind.

Form your own mastermind group of other successful sales professionals.

Structure your selling process so that each stage either answers a question or solves a problem of the customer.

Be prepared to make multiple calls on multiple decision-makers to make major sales. There are no shortcuts.

Set standards of excellent performance for every key skill you need to succeed.

Don't waste valuable selling time with people who are negative or uninterested in your offer.

Do as much research on the client as you can prior to your first meeting. This is very impressive.

Help the customer determine his buying criteria. On what bases will the decision be made?

Keep asking yourself, "What is the most valuable use of my time right now?"

Compare your product continually with those of higher price or lower quality.

Use your time wisely; it is your most precious resource and the only thing you really have to sell.

Apply the "magic of listening" in every sales relationship; listening builds trust.

Lean forward, nod, smile and agree; become fully engaged in the sales conversation.

Sell the future benefit and enjoyment of your product or service; this arouses both anticipation and desire.

Never give in to the temptation to clear up small things first.

Decide how you want your customers to think about you and talk about you when you're not there. Then act accordingly.

Identify your key result areas, those areas where successful outputs are necessary.

Aim for maximum return on selling time; every minute spent in planning saves 10 minutes in execution, a 1,000 percent return!

Practice single-handling with every task; once you start, stay with the job until it's complete.

"Act as if" you were already the person you want most to be.

Be the best! Work at least as hard on yourself as you do on your job.

Aim for meaningful differentiation by emphasizing your "unique selling proposition" continually.

Invest in yourself; continuous learning is the minimum requirement for success in selling.

Achieve mega-credibility by backing your products and services with guarantees and assurances.

Approach sales as a profession, with a specific methodology and process. You will get out of it what you put into it.

Continual review enables you to analyze every part of your sales activities and make a point to improve each one.

Focus on demonstrating suitability and appropriateness rather than high quality or low price.

See yourself as the president of your own personal sales corporation. Introduce a total quality program for everything you do.

Move quickly and continuously. Increase your likelihood of success by increasing the number of your activities.

Just think! You can learn anything you need to achieve any goal you set for yourself. There are no limits.

Be prepared to ride the cycles and trends of life; success is never permanent and failure is never final.

Achieve financial independence by becoming very good in selling, earning good money, and then by holding on to the money.

Pay yourself first; put away 10 percent of every paycheck and resolve to never spend it, for any reason.

Pay attention to the details in selling.
Everything counts!

Think like a psychologist; customers decide emotionally and justify logically.

Identify the deep, emotional needs in your customers that cause them to buy your products or services.

Use low-pressure, no-pressure selling techniques to relax your customer and build trust.

Use strong opening statements to arouse curiosity and arrest attention.

Never argue about price; always look for the reasons behind price objections.

Set priorities on your time and always concentrate on high-value tasks.

Decide to increase your sales by 26 percent per year; that's only 1/2 percent per week, 2 percent per month. Anyone can do that.

Break the preoccupation
of the prospect by asking
a good question aimed at
the result or benefit of
your product.

Ask two questions after every call: "What did I do right?" and "What would I do differently?"

Expect the best! Always look for the good in every situation.

Ask yourself, "Is what I am doing right now leading to a sale?"

Close the sale by saying, "...and I'll take care of all the details."

Always think about the second and third sale while you are working on the first sale.

Tell the customer two or three things about your company of which you are really proud.

Always speak positively about your customers' current suppliers.

Your success in selling will be in direct proportion to what you do after you do what you are expected to do.

About the author

The author of this great little book spent 30 years, traveling in 80 countries, searching for the real reasons why things happen the way they do. Over a period of years, these principles have been taught to thousands of people all over the world. Countless men and women have applied them to their lives, dramatically increasing their levels of health, happiness and prosperity. Brian lives with his wife Barbara and their four children in San Diego, California. He continues to write and teach these timeless principles throughout the world.